EMERGING LEADERS

AN ANNOTATED BIBLIOGRAPHY

EMERGING LEADERS

AN ANNOTATED BIBLIOGRAPHY

Jennifer J. Deal
Karen Peterson
Heidi Gailor-Loflin

Center for Creative Leadership
Greensboro, North Carolina

The Center for Creative Leadership is an international, nonprofit educational institution founded in 1970 to advance the understanding, practice, and development of leadership for the benefit of society worldwide. As a part of this mission, it publishes books and reports that aim to contribute to a general process of inquiry and understanding in which ideas related to leadership are raised, exchanged, and evaluated. The ideas presented in its publications are those of the author or authors.

The Center thanks you for supporting its work through the purchase of this volume. If you have comments, suggestions, or questions about any CCL Press publication, please contact John R. Alexander, President, at the address given below.

Center for Creative Leadership
Post Office Box 26300
Greensboro, North Carolina 27438-6300

Center for
Creative Leadership
leadership. learning. life.

CCL No. 352

Library of Congress Cataloging-in-Publication Data

Deal, Jennifer J.
    Emerging leaders : an annotated bibliography / Jennifer J. Deal, Karen Peterson, Heidi Gailor-Loflin.
      p. cm.
    Includes bibliographical references and indexes.
    ISBN 1-882197-65-8
    1. Leadership—Bibliography. 2. Executives—Bibliography. 3. Generation X—Bibliography. I. Peterson, Karen. II. Gailor-Loflin, Heidi. III. Title.

Z7164.L38 D43 2001
016.6584—dc21
                                       2001025329

Table of Contents

Preface

In the past decade a new generation has been entering the workforce in ever-greater numbers. Because the Center for Creative Leadership (CCL) wants to understand the challenges of working with this new generation and wants to help organizations better understand how to effectively harness the unique skills and talents of this generation, it began a research project in 1999 to examine a series of questions around generational challenges in the workforce, different conceptions of leadership, differences in values, and the changing work contract.

To aid in research, development, and training initiatives, the authors of this CCL Press publication began to identify and collect what literature existed on the topic of emerging leaders in general, and on generational conflict, leadership, values, and the psychological work contract in particular. We consulted scientific and professional journals, articles published in the popular press, books, and World Wide Web sources. The information we collected was so helpful to us that we decided that it could also benefit others. Therefore, we are providing our initial gathering of knowledge and understanding about emerging leaders in this annotated bibliography.

Our understanding of issues relevant to emerging leaders and to working with emerging leaders would not be possible without the foundation provided by the forty-five sources we review in this sourcebook. We are grateful to the writers, researchers, and thinkers whose labor and expertise we have annotated here.

We specifically wish to thank the members of our project team who provided support and their thoughts: Tammy Allen, David Baldwin, Rebecca Bond, Ross DePinto, Sherine Ebadi, David Jacobson, Dana McDonald-Mann, Karissa McKenna, Stephanie Trovas, and Ellen Van Velsor. David Berke, Maura Stevenson, and Douglas Quartetti provided invaluable comments in reviewing an early draft of the manuscript. Thanks also go to Pete Scisco for his editorial guidance.

Introduction

In an increasingly competitive, global, and technology-driven market-place, organizations keep a constant vigil over their management ranks. The ability to recruit, train, develop, and retain workers who can rise to leadership positions is essential to success – even survival – in such a climate. That ability is always challenged by such changes as shifting demographics and technological developments. One specific challenge currently facing organizations is the task of developing leaders from the newest generation of managers. To understand the challenges of working with this new generation and to effectively harness its skills and talents, organizations should begin with three facts: (1) there are fewer managers to choose from and develop among this generation because there are fewer people in this age group than in the generation that preceded it; (2) evolving employment patterns have affected worker attitudes toward employers; and (3) the newest generation of managers has a view toward authority that is different from previous generations, which affects its attitude toward leadership.

Recent and ongoing demographic studies and population research indicate that currently there are too few people in the management population group this publication defines as *emerging leaders* – those rising managers from the generation born between 1964 and 1978 (and labeled in the press as "Generation X"). While in the past there has been a suitable number of adequately trained workers from which organizations could select candidates for managerial and leadership positions, there are currently too few workers with the appropriate skills necessary for taking on the critical leadership challenges companies face. This is partly a result of the United States' robust economic period during the latter half of the 1990s, which provided more work and pulled more people into the workplace but couldn't by itself make workers more competent or better trained. Basic demography also plays a part: there are fewer people in Generation X than there are in the Baby Boom generation (those born between 1946 and 1963). The accelerated rise of the technology industry during the 1990s is yet another factor. This new industry has created a new place for younger workers, spreading (and so reducing) the number of workers available for leadership positions across "old economy" and "new economy" companies.

In addition to the difficulty organizations are having finding younger workers, the standard employment pattern has been changing since the early 1970s. For example, employees no longer expect to stay with the same company for an entire career. Younger workers especially have little expectation of remaining with one company for life, or even for ten years. Hanging on to emerging leaders over the long term has become a serious concern for many organizations. Another change in employment patterns is a shift away from younger people reporting to older people and a move toward younger people being promoted above older people. In some industries and in some competitive environments (the Internet marketplace, for example), organizations perceive that younger employees have skills and abilities that older workers don't. These changes frequently cause generational conflict in organizations.

Finally, Generation X employees have a drastically different view of authority than previous generations. While past generations might have at least acknowledged positional authority, this new generation has little respect for and less interest in leaders who are unable to demonstrate that they can personally produce. In other words, this generation doesn't define *leading* as sitting in meetings and making profound vision statements, but instead as eliminating obstacles and giving employees what they need to work well and comfortably.

The purpose of this publication is to provide an introduction to the current thinking about and the relevant research into emerging leaders and two new generational groups: Generations X and Y. In particular, we want to examine the special needs and issues surrounding these groups as organizations look to develop their younger workers for leadership positions. Our own research in this area focuses on four questions that draw from CCL's long-standing attention to leadership development and which are particularly important to understanding how organizations can retain and develop these current generations of emerging leaders.

1. What are the leadership development needs of emerging leaders, and how do their needs differ from those of other age groups?

2. What are the learning styles of emerging leaders, and how do they differ from those of other age groups?

3. What are the challenges emerging leaders face in defining and shaping their careers?

4. What are the leadership challenges in working across generations?

To help readers navigate this publication we have divided it into three sections. In the "On Emerging Leaders" section we outline the main topics, issues, and themes reflected in the relevant literature, organizing our discussion along the lines of our four research questions. Along with this overview we present suggestions and observations regarding working with and retaining emerging leaders. We base these remarks on our understanding of the literature and on our experience in carrying out our own research into the topic of emerging leaders.

The annotations themselves are arranged in alphabetical order (by author) in a second section. In a separate section we also provide a list of current, relevant Web sites. Author and title indices at the end of the book provide other access points to the source material.

This publication is for individuals who work with, lead, manage, follow, or interact with emerging leaders who are part of the Generation X or Y population groups. It's also recommended for human resources professionals who have been charged with hiring emerging leaders or who manage retention or development efforts related to emerging leaders.

On Emerging Leaders – Attitudes, Development, and Retention

Any deep exploration into the published work related to emerging leaders uncovers a pattern of general themes. It also reveals that specific, tested recommendations based on research – even reliable research itself – are sparse. The themes carried through the current literature suggest strategies based primarily on the experiences consultants, reporters, and scholars have encountered when working with the latest generations of workers. They express different observations, solutions, and approaches, but not all of these results are based on strict empirical evidence or even on extensive fieldwork.

That gap partly fuels CCL's research into this area. Based on the reported work in the field, it's difficult to support strong, specific conclusions about the differences emerging leaders carry with them into the workplace, the practices organizations should employ to develop this new generation of managers, or the most successful tactics organizations can use to retain this generation of workers. Caveats aside, reporting these themes, strategies, and suggestions related to emerging leaders can conceivably benefit anyone who has to work with, lead, manage, follow, interact with, develop, or retain emerging leaders or members of the Generation X or Y population. It can also act as a prelude to more substantial research. The discussion that follows begins at the broadest point, highlighting background information, values, generational conflict, and other issues related to emerging leaders. It then follows the themes revealed through our review of the literature to examine more specific topics, such as management, leadership, and development, as they relate to these newest managerial generations.

Overview

In the late 1980s the popular press began printing stories about the newest generation to enter the workforce, *Generation X*. In the early 1990s this coverage expanded to include the next generational group, then dubbed *Generation Y*. The reporting characterized Generation X members as downtrodden, uninspiring, and self-involved. A series of popular films and books reinforced this stereotype through their descriptions of the changing culture of young Americans.

Since this discussion began in the early 1990s, attempts have been made to understand the defining characteristics of Generation X. Those attempts have usually failed. There is no shortage of characterizing and psychoanalyzing Generation X, but reliable data on the group remain rare. A few demographic studies, however, show that Generation X members do share some characteristics (Conger, 1998; Holtz, 1995; Losyk, 1997; Munk, 1999; Raines, 1997; Smith & Clurman, 1997):

- they are more diverse in ethnicity, more accepting of different perspectives, and more educated than previous generations

- they were more likely than previous generations to be latchkey kids, in daycare, with divorced parents, or part of a single-parent household

- they were raised on political scandal and frequently equate organized religion with intolerance

- they began working with technology (computers in particular) at an earlier age than did members of previous generations and so entered the workforce with a high level of proficiency and comfort with computers and other technologies.

Working and Leading Across Generations: Different Values Present Challenges

The popular press has written extensively about generational conflict in the workplace (Is the Boomer/Gen-X war over?, 2000; Kennedy, 1998c; Munk, 1999). It's suggested (largely based on the "Gen Xer" stereotype) that Generation X workers cause much of this conflict because they don't act the way older people would prefer them to act. And while it's true that this could be said of almost any American generation (what, for example, did the Victorians think of their Jazz Age offspring?), the difference is that now (unlike in the past) young people have considerable economic and social power. Not only do they have power, but they use it. They aren't as controllable and can't easily be forced to comply. That causes problems with older workers who think that younger workers should "wait their turn" and "show some respect" for experience. Increasingly, however, organizations are valuing competence over tenure or age.

Some of the current thinking on this difference treats it as a diversity issue (Flynn, 1996; Watkins, 1999). Other writers see it as an authority issue (Raines, 1997). Some companies make the most of generational differences by capitalizing on the perceived strengths of each group – for example, the business savvy of the older group and the energy, foresight, and knowledge of the younger group (Kruger & Mieszkowski, 1998). Almost all of the literature, however, reflects a belief that it's the manager's job to deal with the conflict constructively, even when much of the conflict relates to authority.

Current thinking about the conflict between generations in the work-place pinpoints a difference in values as a primary challenge to working with and leading different generations. But although there's a great deal of attention paid to those differences, few researchers actually pin down specific differences (Craig & Bennett, 1997). We find no writing that reports definitively whether these differences are part of a standard maturational pattern (Costa & McCrae, 1999) or are unique to Generation X (Arnett, 2000). Researchers did find that members of Generation X generally have a more negative attitude toward jobs, shopping, parents, and yuppies than their Baby Boom counterparts (Manolis, Levin, & Dahlstrom, 1997). There is some limited support for the perception that Generation X workers focus more on balanced lifestyle (Bernardi, 1999; Burke, 1994; Joyner, 2000) and want frequent feedback (Burke, 1994). But because these studies don't compare their results with similar data gathered from other generational groups, it's impossible to draw any conclusions about what differences actually exist.

Even without a clear definition of exactly what differences in values are expressed in the emerging leaders population group compared with those in older population groups, evidence suggests that there is a large difference in the way each group expresses its values behaviorally and verbally. In other words, managers directing younger workers may or may not find that they share values, but are likely to see that the way each group expresses those values are markedly different. Conflicts are more likely to be related to behavior than values. Behavior that leads to conflict provides managers with an opportunity to discuss with each side why the behavior is constructive or not to the task at hand and to emphasize the organization's commonly held values.

Building Successful Careers: Loyalty, Retention, and Emerging Leaders

Current reports indicate conclusively that the psychological work contract is different today from what it was twenty or thirty years ago. That contract is the implicit agreement between the employee and the employer – what the employee expects to do for a company, and what the employee expects to get in return (Barner, 1996; Gabriel, 1999; Robinson, Kraatz, & Rousseau, 1994). In contrast to the past, when workers might express an implied loyalty in return for lifetime employment, an employee entering the workforce today doesn't expect to work for one company for an entire career. This radical shift in the psychological work contract affects the approach and attitude employees take toward work and is one of the most frequently discussed differences between the emerging leaders of today and the members of previous generations (Tornow, 1988; Withers, 1998).

The current employment trend among *all* working people is toward a belief that the employer looks on the employee as disposable, that a job is not for life, and that the employer feels no obligation to the employee (De Meuse & Tornow, 1990; Martin, Staines, & Pate, 1998). Much of the published thinking on this topic as it relates to emerging leaders focuses on the idea that members of Generation X feel less loyalty toward their employers than did previous generations (Crainer & Dearlove, 1999). According to the few studies that exist, it's probable that young employees today do feel less obligation to their employers than other generational groups did in the past (Daboval, 1998), but it's unclear whether belonging to a particular generation has much to do with this change (Martin, Staines, & Pate, 1998; Tornow, 1988).

It's also unclear (because researchers have not studied it and other writers have not widely reported on it) how entering the workforce with this perspective affects careers. But certainly the change in the psychological work contract does present challenges to emerging leaders, not only when they enter the workforce but also as they develop in their careers. For example, an employee feels no obligation to be loyal to the employer if that loyalty requires turning down a better offer or staying with an organization when advancement or development isn't as rapid as desired (Tornow, 1988). Emerging leaders may in fact feel less traditional loyalty to their employers in part because of the contrast between the job insecurity that was prevalent as they came of age (lowered expectations) and the boom economy that rose in the mid-1990s (seize every opportunity to advance and to keep working). The free agency concept popularized in professional sports is an apt metaphor for the attitude emerging leaders carry into the workplace – they will stay with an organization as long as it's the best offer on the table.

Organizations also face challenges in the wake of a changed psychological work contract, particularly in the area of retaining emerging leaders so that they can be developed for positions critical to the organization's long-term success. The current economic climate and "war for talent" in the United States and in Europe (Chambers, Foulon, Handfield-Jones, Hankin, & Michaels, 1998) has brought retention to the forefront as an increasingly critical human resources issue (Tornow, 1988). Organizations can adopt any number of tactics to retain Generation X employees in general and emerging leaders in particular (Kupperschmidt, 2000; Swoboda, 1999). Most of these tactics involve nonmonetary reward systems such as vacation time, employee control over schedules, development opportunities, positive reinforcement and acknowledgment from people younger workers respect, coaching, and mentoring (Cole, 1999; Cox, 1999; Kennedy, 1998a; Withers, 1998). Much of the writing on this subject indicates that younger workers also look for life/work balance, vacation time, flexible scheduling, corporate culture, interesting work, and benefits.

Emerging Leaders and Management: Perceptions Toward Leadership

One of the primary conflicts between generations in the workplace lies in the areas of management and leadership (Kincaid, 1998; Watkins, 1999). Those areas touch on values, work contract issues, and the perception of what it means to be a manager or leader (Bertsch, 1996; Woodward, 1999). As this group of emerging leaders has entered the workplace, it has become apparent that there's an important difference between this group and older groups in the way each perceives authority in the workplace and in the way each behaves as managers and leaders in the workplace.

In contrast to previous generations, this group of emerging leaders does not accord people respect simply because of their position (Hays, 1999; Holtz, 1995). Members of Generation X frequently don't acknowledge authority. The literature in this area reveals Generation X's prevailing view toward authority: Don't listen to leaders until they prove they can actually do the work themselves (Holtz, 1995). Unlike workers from previous generations, Generation X workers don't assume authority exists or arises from position (Raines, 1997). If managers can't demonstrate that they can get things done themselves (rather than convince others to carry out the work), then it's unlikely that many members of the Generation X group will grant them the same degree of authority as members of older generational groups will (Kennedy, 1998b; Rapp, 1999). Authority and respect arising from the position an individual occupies just isn't part of this generation's attitude (Raines, 1997). This generation of workers expects its managers to "earn their stripes," regardless of their manager's superior position or longer experience.

That attitude toward authority is frequently taken as an indication of the "disrespect" that the emerging leaders population feels toward its elders in general and bosses in particular. However, many articles consulted for this publication point out that although many people in the workplace view this attitude as disrespectful, it can be more aptly described as skeptical. It's a skepticism that requires a boss to prove that he or she is still capable – skill isn't assumed because of position. This general skepticism may arise from the fact that Generation X came of age without heroes or leaders it could claim as its own (political scandals, for example, removed potential political heroes). It may also be a result of this generation's being raised in a period of heightened consumer marketing that succeeded only in raising suspicion of anything that smacks of "hype" – including perhaps the war stories of "self-made" leaders in the organizations in which they work.

Another explanation for this skeptical view of authority may be rooted in the relative inexperience emerging leaders have in the workplace. In any particular organization, for example, managers of a previous generation may have already proved their technical expertise years before Generation X employees joined the organization. As those older workers shifted from technical to managerial positions they developed leadership skills different from (and as a complement to) the technical skills that carried them through earlier career stages. Newer workers don't see those technical skills and, because of their inexperience in the organization, may assume that they don't exist – which in turn leads them to doubt managerial authority. (Alternatively, technological changes may have, in the emerging leader's view, simply outpaced the older manager's technical skills.)

The emerging leader group from Generation X does appear to respect authenticity and the ability to get things done, so managers leading employees from this group would do well to focus on tactics that communicate authenticity and sincerity in order to get results. Managers may be more effective with Generation X employees by acting as mentors, for example, and developing personal relationships with them to understand what motivates individual employees (Kennedy, 1998b). It appears that this relationship approach to development may be critical to managing Generation X employees, but there's little data to support a definitive statement.

Developing Emerging Leaders: How Learning Styles Differ for Emerging Leaders

Considering the apparent importance of development for retaining emerging leaders (Rapp, 1999; Woodward, 1999), it's surprising that so little has been written about the subject (Ohlott & Eastman, 1994; Tunnicliffe, 1997). Though there is general agreement that this group needs and wants to be developed (Rapp, 1999; Woodward, 1999), there's little reliable research to show what type of development its members need or how to best deliver it to them (Wagschal, 1995).

Despite the lack of research and the absence of agreement regarding developmental tactics, much of the writing about Generation X workers is consistent in arguing that emerging leaders want development. Emerging leaders focus intently on learning new skills in large part because they don't believe in job security (a result of the changing psychological work contract and coming of age in an era of lowered expectations). As a group, emerging leaders believe that learning new skills protects them against layoffs and provides more lucrative job opportunities. Therefore, this group is interested in getting development in areas that they believe will add marketable skills to their portfolio.

One development tactic that does seem to fit this group of younger employees is the use of frequent feedback (Burke, 1994; Salopek, 2000). In addition, managers and organizations can capitalize on the group's drive to gain more marketable skills by providing training that is clear, flexible, self-directed, and entertaining (Caudron, 1997; Knight, 2000; Salopek, 2000). That training doesn't have to be radically different from what is offered to other generational groups – the general techniques discussed in much of the current writing on this topic are those that may work with any group (Salopek, 2000).

Conclusion

Despite the scarcity of reliable research that might help organizations develop specific, tested strategies for recruiting, developing, and retaining emerging leaders, the record of observations and research reflected in the current literature about this subject does reveal a definite thematic pattern of characteristics in the emerging leaders population. That pattern includes attitudes and perceptions this generation holds related to such issues as managerial authority, employer loyalty, developmental opportunities, and the relationships between direct reports and their managers. Organizations can examine that pattern in developing their own approach to recruiting, developing, and retaining emerging leaders.

Annotated Bibliography

The annotations here reflect readings from a wide variety of sources identified through *PsychLit*, *Social Sciences Citation Index*, *ABI Inform*, and the *Melvyl* databases (available at the University of California, San Diego). We searched these databases using author names and such key words as *generational conflict, leadership, management, psychological work contract, values, Generation X, Generation Y*, and *Baby Boomers*. We also gathered recommendations from colleagues, reviewed bibliographic references from particularly relevant articles, and examined conference proceedings. The sources can be characterized as scientific journal articles, articles from the popular press, books, book chapters, essays from practitioners and experts, and a few citations taken from the World Wide Web.

We had several criteria for deciding whether or not to include a citation. For example, the material had to be directly related to one of our primary questions and recently published (almost all sources appeared in print after 1990). Older material had to have a place as a seminal piece of writing on the subject. We specifically included sources that were directly related to the background of our questions, such as sources describing the basis of the psychological work contract or differences in values. Although we looked for academic rigor in the literature we reviewed, we did not exclude writing based on this variable because this area of research is fairly new and because we found most of the articles had been published in the popular press. We did not include sources that didn't reach a conclusion or provide a new perspective, nor did we include those that simply restated what the "classics" in this genre had already reported.

The content of each annotation varies by source. Our general approach was to include the purpose of the material, a brief summary of the contents, what new information was reported, and what conclusion was reached.

Arnett, J. J. (2000). High hopes in a grim world: Emerging adults' view of
    their futures and Generation X. *Youth & Society, 31*(3), 267–286.

This study focused on the views of emerging adults (between the ages
of 21 and 28) regarding their personal futures and the future of their generation (defined as *Generation X*). The results showed that the young adults were
optimistic about their own futures and believed their lives would be as good
as or better than their parents' lives. They believed that financial gain was
important, but not as important as realizing their hopes and dreams for the
future. This was especially true in respondents whose parents were financially
successful. The young adults also placed a high value on personal relationships and planned to have better personal relationships and fewer divorces
than their parents. While the respondents had high hopes for their personal
futures, they also believed that in general their generation was cynical and
pessimistic. They reported that education was not synonymous with finding a
fulfilling occupation and expressed concern about crime and social problems.

✵✵✵

Barner, R. (1996). The new millennium workplace: Several changes that will
    challenge managers and workers. *Futurist, 30*(2), 14–18.

The writer contended that there are seven trends that will reshape the
work environment over the next ten years: (1) the move to virtual organizations, (2) the shift to a just-in-time workforce, (3) the rise of the knowledge
worker, (4) the computerization of mentoring and coaching, (5) the continued
growth of diversity, (6) the aging of the workforce, and (7) the creation of a
more dynamic workforce. These changes will demand managers who are
flexible to changing environments. According to the article, as these trends
evolve managers will need to develop the ability to respond rapidly, focus
precisely, manage stress, think strategically, juggle staff, and build teams.

✵✵✵

Bernardi, L. M. (1999). Balancing act: The strategic benefits and legal neces-
    sity of the work/home life balance. *Canadian Manager, 24*(4), 10–12.

In this article Bernardi focused on the greatest source of employee
stress – the desire to balance a work and personal life. He argued that this
focus on balance is due to many families having dual incomes, which obvi-
ates the issue of childcare, and company downsizing efforts that have affected
employee job security and loyalty.

The author wrote that work/home life balance, as a strategic human
resource issue, can help attract and retain valuable employees. As the job
market has shifted, employees have demanded more from organizations. They

see work as only one aspect of their lives, and they want time for life outside of work. The author noted several actions that organizations and managers can take to attract and retain employees, prevent discrimination lawsuits, and have happier and more productive workers. Organizations can allow alternative work arrangements and offer family-friendly benefits. The manager's role is to promote and support those family-friendly policies.

✻✻✻

Bertsch, J. (1996). Bringing Xers aboard. *Getting Results . . . for the Hands-On Manager, 41*(12), 1–2.

This article provided tips for helping managers hire and manage Generation Xers. It suggested that employers focus on skills rather than years of service because Generation Xers want to build their portfolio of marketable skills and, once hired, they seek opportunities to build their skills and develop their talents. This generation of workers also demands to know the overall vision and mission of their organization so they can place their work in a broader context. They also seek clear communications. According to the article, employers looking to hire from this pool of workers should build on this generation's inherent skill sets. These workers are comfortable with technology, are able to multitask, and have a cosmopolitan view of the world. To keep Generation Xers, employers must reward them not only with financial incentives but also with such perks as vacation time.

✻✻✻

Burke, R. J. (1994). Generation X: Measures, sex and age differences. *Psychological Reports, 74*(2), 555–562.

The data reported in this article provided some limited support for the popular depiction of Generation X members as focused on a balanced lifestyle and wanting frequent feedback. The researchers found that the values expressed by women were more consistent with the stereotype of Generation X, and that both men and women expressed such views as valuing high ethical standards and being concerned about the environment. Older women and men expressed values that were less consistent with the stereotype of Generation X. Because the study did not include subjects from outside of Generation X, it was not able to conclude whether the attitudes reported were a result of an age or generational orientation or were more generally held in society.

✻✻✻

Caudron, S. (1997). Can Generation Xers be trained? *Training & Development, 51*(3), 20–25.

This article focused on the training needs of Generation X, the group of forty million Americans who in 1997 were between the ages of twenty and thirty-three. The article reported that companies are re-creating their training programs to meet the learning preferences, values, communication styles, and experiences of Generation X. To appeal to Generation Xers, the author said training should be entertaining, experiential, focused on outcomes, clear, flexible, and self-directed. Computers are an appropriate choice for delivering training to this generation because its members were reared on technology. In addition to discussing training styles, the author stated that this generation views training as a key benefit, which means companies can view training as critical for attracting, retaining, and motivating the workers in this generational group.

✳✳✳

Chambers, E. G., Foulon, M., Handfield-Jones, H., Hankin, S. M., & Michaels, E. G., III. (1998). The war for talent. *The McKinsey Quarterly, 3*, 44–57.

Big U.S. companies are finding it difficult to attract and retain good people, according to the authors of this article. They indicated that the war for talent can be won if organizations elevate talent management to a corporate priority.

The authors argued that there has been a wide-ranging shortage in talent, and it will continue through 2003. During that time the supply of suitable employees will shrink for several reasons: women are no longer surging into the workforce, white-collar productivity improvements have flattened, immigration levels are stable, and executives are not prolonging their careers. Companies face three qualitative challenges in the battle for talent: (1) a more complex economy demands more sophisticated talent, (2) the emergence of efficient capital markets in the United States has increased competition through the rise of many small and medium-size companies, and (3) job mobility has increased.

To meet these challenges, the authors wrote, organizations must be clear about the kinds of people that are good for them, use a range of innovative channels to bring those people into the organization, and have organizational commitment to getting the best talent available. The article included tips for organizations that want to aggressively develop talent, including putting people in jobs before they're ready, putting a good feedback system in place, understanding the scope of their retention problem, and taking immediate action on poor performers.

According to research, executive talent has been the most undermanaged corporate asset for the 1980s and 1990s. Therefore, organizations must make talent management a priority if they are to survive.

✳✳✳

Cole, J. (1999). The art of wooing Gen Xers. *HR Focus*, *76*(11), 7–8.

Cole defined Generation Xers as those born between 1965 and 1981. They grew up during the computer revolution, the advent of MTV, business downsizings, and massive layoffs. All this and more influenced what Generation X is and what it expects to get from the workplace.

In analyzing Gen Xers' work habits, Cole reported that they are not unmotivated and lazy as they were first categorized. Gen Xers instead seek fun and meaning in their work. They have come to expect huge salaries, are not interested in retirement plans, and do not feel a sense of loyalty to employers. They require short-term rewards and constant feedback. They are also more comfortable with diversity and global issues.

Cole wrote that companies can attract, hire, retain, and manage Generation X workers with such tactics as career workshops, 360-degree-feedback surveys, psychological profiling, and individual counseling. Cole cautioned that managers can't focus on the individuality of each worker regardless of their generational idiosyncrasies. Organizations need a "one policy fits all" set of management objectives.

Cole concluded with ten tips for managing Gen Xers by Michael Sullivan, president of 50-Plus Communications Consulting.

1. Challenge Gen Xers with assignments that allow them to use their entrepreneurial and pragmatic skills.

2. Use employee interaction to create a team spirit.

3. Build their confidence by letting them use their problem-solving abilities.

4. Explain the pros and cons of business initiatives and outcomes.

5. Show Gen Xers how their work is important to the organization and how their work relates to other areas in the organization.

6. Encourage Gen Xers to participate in the planning process of their organizational unit.

7. Give clear directions and explain the rationale behind your directions.

8. Pair Gen Xers with older workers.

9. Show Gen Xers potential career paths in the organization.

10. Provide Gen Xers with immediate feedback, including a rational explanation.

✳✳✳

Conger, J. A. (1998). How 'Gen X' managers manage. *Business and Strategy*, *10*, 21–31.

Generation X managers are different from those in the Baby Boom generation, according to Conger. They are more skeptical, for example, and have different values. In this article Conger explored the Silent Generation (born between 1925 and 1942), the Baby Boomers (born between 1943 and 1964), and Generation X (born between 1965 and 1981), describing what makes each generation unique – from the manner in which it was raised to the world events that shaped its views. He then explored the challenges facing workers of different generations as they take their views and attitudes into the workplace.

Conger concluded with an outline of four prominent traits found among Generation Xers that have implications for today's workforce: (1) their quest for a real balance between work and private life, (2) their sense of independence, (3) their intimacy with technology and information, and (4) their desire for a workplace that feels like a community.

✳✳✳

Costa, P. T., & McCrae, R. R. (1999). Personalities across cultures: Studies focused on age factors. *Aging Today*, *20*(2), 5.

Costa used the Revised NEO Personality Inventory (NEO-pi-r) to look at personality traits across life spans. This assessment instrument has been used to make cross-sectional comparisons of adolescents and older adults across several different cultures. Research in the United States and Canada has provided evidence of age differences in personality between adolescence and age thirty. College-age individuals continually score lower than older adults on conscientiousness and agreeableness; however, they score higher on neuroticism, extroversion, and openness. Adults in North America were reported as being less emotional and inquisitive but more socially responsible than their adolescent counterparts. In other cultures, research using the NEO-pi-r has shown the same age trends – a decline in neuroticism, extroversion, and openness, and an increase in agreeableness and conscientiousness as people mature.

This research showed that scores increased over time. Age differences in conscientiousness appeared to be due to maturational changes. It appeared there were universal age changes, which were biologically based, perhaps because of genetic influences on personality traits.

***

Cox, J. A. (1999). What's happening in the workplace? *Baylor Business Review, 17*(2), 7–8.

Cox addressed how managers and organizations can deal with an aging population and adapt to work and family issues. In this article he reported that as Baby Boomers head toward retirement they are not easily adapting to the change. Medical advancements have led to longer life spans and a better quality of life, and labor laws have changed so that most jobs no longer have a mandatory retirement age. At age forty, workers are protected by the Age Discrimination in Employment Act. The challenge for the manager of retiring Baby Boomers is in designing more flexible work plans for the aging worker, which might include flexible scheduling, part-time work, reduced hours with reduced pay, and job sharing.

The author also reported a growing desire for work/life balance among all employees. Successful organizations recognize that workers want to have balance in all areas of their lives, and can increase productivity by treating employees as "whole" individuals with lives beyond the workplace. He described how companies are beginning to address the work/life balance issues through the use of such services and benefits as job sharing, part-time employment, the compressed workweek, home-based employment, adoption benefits, childcare, eldercare, wellness programs, and employee-assistance programs.

***

Craig, S. C., & Bennett, S. E. (Eds.). (1997). *After the boom: The politics of Generation X.* Lanham, MD: Rowman & Littlefield, 212 pages.

This collection of articles was based on a broad array of data. The editors agreed that generational analysis is an inexact science at best, and that the conclusions the contributors reached need to be tested by time. They went on to draw a few general conclusions. One, it's reasonable that observers report differences between Baby Boomers and Generation Xers because the world in which each generation came of age was different for Boomers than for Gen Xers, and this difference has had an effect on each generation's views and attitudes. The second conclusion the data suggested was that these differences are not as large as they have been made out to be; namely, that

Gen Xers display a pattern of beliefs similar to those of older groups. The third conclusion was that though the differences between the generations may not be as exaggerated as the popular press has made them out to be, they are large enough to cause significant difficulties in work settings. The editors argued that managers need to pay attention to how fundamental differences between the generations, such as those related to autonomy and tolerance, have affected, and continue to affect, the workplace.

✻✻✻

Crainer, S., & Dearlove, D. (1999). Death of executive talent. *Management Review*, *88*(7), 8–13.

The authors predicted that organizations will be scrambling to find qualified managers and executives through the year 2050. There are fewer young people moving up in the ranks, and Baby Boomers and the Silent Generation are retiring. Mergers and downsizings have also caused employees to leave. As the pool of potential managers has shrunk, the qualifications and skills needed to become a senior executive have changed and increased in scope. Companies now expect more from executives, especially organizations thinking about a global expansion.

Generation X, wrote the authors, is part of a potential pool of current and future leaders. This generation's members generally distrust hierarchy, prefer to be evaluated based on merit rather than status, are less "loyal" to the company they work for (meaning they are prepared to look for other employment opportunities if their needs are not being met), and have their own agenda. In an attempt to address some of the issues that arise from the combination of increased attrition and demographic changes in the workforce, the authors devised a succession plan. It included such tactics as working to understand individuals and growing talent on the inside.

✻✻✻

Daboval, J. M. (1998). *A comparison between Baby Boomer and Generation X employees' bases and foci of commitment.* Unpublished doctoral dissertation, Nova Southeastern University, Ft. Lauderdale, FL.

This unpublished dissertation reported the results of an investigation into whether Boomer and Generation X employees shared the same level and placement of commitment to their employers. According to the author, the level of commitment targeted either to the supervisor or to the organization was higher for Boomers than for Generation X employees. The study suggested that the traditional forms of commitment through identification with supervisor or internalization of organizational objectives do not hold with Generation X, and that their level of commitment may be more strongly related to human resource policies such as development and reward systems. The author argued that just because Generation X employees' commitment is nontraditional, it shouldn't be construed to mean that they are incapable of commitment.

According to the author's report, members of the Baby Boom generation and Generation X develop attitudes to commitment that are specific to the economic, political, and social events that took place during their formative years. These attitudes were a significant part of organizational culture and employee attitudes. Baby Boomers show more commitment to organizations than do Generation Xers. For Generation X employees, commitment was seemingly weighted to professional development, benefits, and practices that improve a worker's personal marketability. On the whole, Generation X employees appeared to exercise greater independence in the workplace because they focused on personal development, personal accountability, and improving their bank of skills.

✳✳✳

De Meuse, K. P., & Tornow, W. W. (1990). The tie that binds–has become very, very frayed! *Human Resource Planning*, *13*(3), 203–213.

This article described the changing work contract, explained why the work contract is changing, demonstrated what some of the changes are, and made suggestions and recommendations for how employers can adapt to these changes. The authors reported that the work contract has moved from what could be characterized as stability, permanence, and predictability, with full-time work and lifetime employment, to a situation in which constant change, impermanence, and uncertainty are common, and full-time work and lifetime employment are uncommon. This change in the unwritten employment contract has resulted in many employees adopting a "free agent" mentality, expecting to be paid for performance and skills rather than for tenure and loyalty.

The authors suggested that to meet this change employers need to change their staffing practices to be more flexible, shift their compensation systems to reflect pay for performance rather than pay for tenure, modify their training to focus more on life and career planning rather than skills development, and adopt termination practices that are more considerate of the company's long-term, rather than short-term, needs. The authors concluded that both employees and employers can benefit from the new implicit work contract, but only if each pays attention and deals with the new situation rather than bemoaning the loss of the old.

✳✳✳

Flynn, G. (1996). Xers vs. Boomers: Teamwork or trouble? *Personnel Journal*, *75*(11), 86–90.

This article focused on the conflicts between generations in the workplace and how human resources departments can provide work environments that meet the needs of both Generation Xers and Baby Boomers. The apparent conflict between the two generations in the workplace is due at least in part to their desire for different benefits. The author suggested that human resources departments allow for some differences in desired benefits – that a one-size benefit package can no longer fit every employee. Generation Xers look for childcare, for example, while Boomers look to plan financially for retirement. Human resources departments should customize information about benefits to the needs of the different generations. The company should talk about the needs and issues pertaining to various age groups. In fact, reported the author, open communication about age differences can allow for better communication between the generations.

✳✳✳

Gabriel, A. R. (1999). Retaining Gen Xers: Not such a mystery anymore. *Commercial Law Bulletin*, *14*(4), 32–33.

To establish a long, productive relationship with Generation X employees and to retain them, the author suggested that managers adapt their skills to meet the needs of those they are managing. Demographically, Xers are accustomed to working independently, rapidly incorporating information, multitasking, and continuously learning in an effort to maximize their marketability in an uncertain world. Additionally, this group wants increased autonomy, additional mentoring rather than what they see as "micromanagement," regular and appropriate feedback, and rewards to acknowledge the attainment of every goal. Managers can satisfy this group's appetite for new challenges by providing growth opportunities; members of Generation X look for an organization and a manager who will work with them and help them to continue to grow and develop with the company, not just for it.

✳✳✳

Hays, S. (1999). Generation X and the art of the reward. *Workforce, 78*(11), 44–48.

The author wrote that members of Generation X are an important part of most organizations, but that it is a challenge motivating and retaining them. This generation was described as self-reliant and having an entrepreneurial spirit. According to the author, Generation Xers commit themselves to a work/life balance and are more likely than those of other generations to leave an employer for a more challenging job. They tend to be more financially engaged and oriented toward work, but they also want flexibility and freedom. They have described themselves as technologically savvy, aggressive, cynical, and realistic; they say they want to be involved in decision making; and they want accurate and timely feedback.

Hays outlined six nonfinancial rewards identified by Bruce Tulgan as suitable for Gen Xers: (1) more control over their own schedules, (2) access to learning marketable skills, (3) exposure to decision-makers, (4) the chance to put their names on tangible results, (5) clear areas of responsibility, and (6) creative freedom.

✳✳✳

Holtz, G. T. (1995). *Welcome to the jungle: The why behind Generation X.* New York: St. Martin's Press, 289 pages.

This book described the world that people born between 1960 and 1980 grew up in and the impact that world has had on the development of those people. Rather than calling them "Generation X," Holtz called people born during this time period the "Free Generation." Using sociological data, newspaper clippings, real-life experiences, anecdotes, and a wide variety of statistics, Holtz highlighted how different the world was when this group grew up compared to the world in which earlier generations grew up. This book offered a thorough description of the cultural, political, and economic forces that shaped this generation. Holtz concluded that the behaviors seen in members of Generation X – and which others describe as self-centered, disinterested, disconnected, and rude – are reasonable given the world they grew up in.

✳✳✳

Is the Boomer/Gen-X war over? (2000). *HR Focus, 77*(5), 1–13.

This article described findings from J. Walker Smith's research, which he presented at the Work-Life 2000 Conference in New York. It focused on the idea that there really is not a gap between Generation X and Baby Boomers in reference to work/life balance and career issues.

Smith examined two generations active in the workforce today: Boomers and Generation Xers. As defined in this article, Boomers were born between 1936 and 1954. They value individuality and youth and are self-absorbed. Generation Xers were born after 1955. They are savvy and entrepreneurial and value diversity. Smith discussed some of the societal influences that helped shape both generations. Smith indicated that the values Boomers and Xers hold are beginning to meld. Boomers have softened their view of work and begun placing more value on living the good life, for example, as Generation Xers value competition and hard work.

Smith noted some trends among the general working public, and Gen Xers in particular, that will continue to evolve. These include such ideas as lifestyles coming before work, empowerment as key to motivating employees, and women having more power in the workplace. The free-agent worker mentality, which Smith argued was born among the Gen Xers, will take hold in both generations.

The article also described Smith's presentation of preliminary findings from "Ask the Children 2000: Youth and Employment," a study of 1,028 high school students conducted by the Families and Work Institute. Eighty percent of the students surveyed expected to complete at least a four-year degree, and 31 percent expected to complete some postgraduate education. Almost all of the students planned to have a paid job at some point after completing their education. Forty percent wanted to work for a large organization. The students felt potential employers will be seeking such skills as the ability to get a job done, even when the tasks are not well defined; being able to work under pressure and meet deadlines; and finding a creative way to do a job better or faster. The aspects of future jobs that mattered to the students included meaningful work that offers security, allows time for personal or family activities, provides good benefits, offers the chance to work with people who treat them well, and is a place where they can have fun. The study also noted the lessons students have learned about work: the importance of hard work, the importance of working with people who are different from themselves, and the importance of a life outside of work.

＊＊＊

Joyner, T. (2000). Gen X-ers focus on life outside the job, fulfillment. *Secured Lender, 56*(3), 64–68.

Baby Boomers defined and redefined work for the last quarter of the twentieth century. They invented double-income families and perfected the 50-hour workweek, off-the-scale productivity, and office politics. Members of Generation X are also serious about work, but they don't take it or themselves too seriously. Joyner defined Gen Xers as those born between 1964 and 1980. They tend toward getting the job done and going home to their personal lives. Joyner interviewed several young people who are in school or just starting work. They want flexibility, money, and benefits; a harmonious work environment; identity; and fulfillment in the workplace.

* * *

Kennedy, M. M. (1998a). Boomers vs. busters. *Healthcare Executive*, *13*(6), 6–10.

The author discussed how important it is for healthcare organizations to attend to age diversity. Since 2000 there were five generational groups in the workplace: Pre-Boomer (born 1935–1945), Boomer (born 1946–1959), Cusper (born 1960–1965), Buster (born 1965–1975), and Post-TV (born 1975–1981). Each of these groups differs significantly in terms of its values, lifestyle, motivation, communication skills, perspective on the role of the manager, orientation to teamwork, organizational loyalty, and its ranking of the importance of technical competence. These differences can lead to misunderstanding and conflict among the generations.

Older generations tend to be motivated more by money, while the younger generations prefer time off and skill development, argued the author. Younger generations tend to be more frank and questioning, while the older generations tend to be more polite and affirming. When managing these different age groups it's important to realize that each generation brings a unique set of skills to the organization. Organizations must learn to customize training and communications to capitalize on those skills.

* * *

Kennedy, M. M. (1998b). The extras Xers want. *Across the Board*, *35*(6), 51–52.

Kennedy conducted a focus group of Generation Xers to offer human resource managers insights into developing the best benefits package for attracting this group of employees. Perks that Generation Xers considered desirable included more time off, unpaid leave, telecommuting, flexible schedules, independent health insurance, retirement plans, technical training, and mentoring. Members of the Generation X group weren't excited by such perks as company social events, first-class tickets, excellent hotels, and fine dining.

* * *

Kennedy, M. M. (1998c). The new rules. *Across the Board, 35*(2), 51–52.

This article gave some ideas and tips for Baby Boomers managing younger workers. They included:

1. Practice leadership and not management. Younger workers want to learn from their managers.

2. Don't forget the importance of direct reports.

3. Relationships count because younger workers depend on relationships over positional power.

4. Inclusion is critical to younger workers who want their ideas to matter.

5. Exhibit and ask for both modesty and consideration. Younger workers won't tolerate arrogance.

6. Be mindful of lavish spending because younger workers dislike waste.

7. Act early on rumors of discontent; don't let problems fester.

8. Understand the importance of young allies. They give good references and have helped many of their managers find new jobs.

9. Be responsive to voice mail.

10. Don't expect younger employees to seek promotions as readily as older workers. They get more satisfaction out of knowing they're making a difference.

✳✳✳

Kincaid, A. (1998). Helm dwellers: A look at the changing nature of non-profit leadership. *Foundation News and Commentary*. Retrieved July 5, 2000, from the World Wide Web: http://int1.cof.org/foundationnews/NovDec98/HelmDwellers.html

According to the author, the changing world of work calls for a new type of leader who is responsive and able to find the most expedient way of getting the job done. Kincaid indicated that members of Generation X might be the best fit for this call to leadership. These emerging leaders bring energy, enthusiasm, and naïveté, qualities that allow young leaders to aim high and meet goals. It's a generation that is familiar with technology, is comfortable with diversity, encourages collaboration, is committed to volunteerism, and possesses an entrepreneurial outlook.

Leadership, in Kincaid's context, incorporates new ways of doing things. It involves collaboration, cooperation, and agreement. The author outlined old and new leadership styles. Old leadership styles included talking, deciding, zero-sum politics, arguing, debating, exclusivity, nervousness about diversity, deciding what to do about issues, and hoarding power. The new leadership styles included listening, empowering, win-win politics, collaborating, finding common ground, openness, comfort with diversity, framing issues, and sharing power.

✳✳✳

Knight, J. (2000). Generation Y: How to train it and retain it. *Restaurant Hospitality*, *84*(5), 88–90.

Based on hiring, training, and retaining tips from the Hard Rock Café restaurant chain, Knight presented advice for managers. The author suggested that managers think visually when training members of younger generations because members of those groups respond better to visual training. The author also suggested that managers balance different training methods to keep younger workers from becoming bored. Immediate feedback reinforces behavior better than delayed feedback. Managers should also emphasize the fun in training and help employees understand the benefits available when working in their particular organization. Finally, the author suggested that a good understanding of the younger generation's perspectives will better position organizations to train and retain frontline employees.

✳✳✳

Kruger, P., & Mieszkowski, K. (1998). Stop the fight. *Fast Company,* Issue 17, 93–111.

This article profiled four leaders who work in computer and Internet companies in which different generations work together. Each profile detailed the individual's best practices for working in organizations that are made up of individuals in their twenties and forties. One individual suggested that experience counts and that organizations need to balance younger and older workers – that older employees bring vision and business knowledge, and younger staff bring technology know-how. To help the two generations work better together, the article reported, it's important to provide mentoring and demand discipline and a longer-term perspective from all employees.

Another executive, the youngest in the organization, suggested that younger employees bring enthusiasm and drive to corporations, but this needs to be tempered by a healthy respect for staff. A third executive stated that older employees need to show that they will take on the same challenges as younger staff and show the same amount of dedication to bringing projects out on schedule. The fourth executive suggested that for different generations to work successfully side by side, organizations must value compromise between the generations and encourage a healthy respect for differences in style.

This article also described how four companies have dealt with the cultural conflict between workers in their twenties and workers in their forties. Using specific examples from I-Village, Philips Mobile Computing Group, Sony Online Entertainment, and I-Traffic, the article pointed out how each group can learn from the other. The discussion focused on specific developmental opportunities for both groups, including "radical mentoring" for the younger group and "earning your stripes" for the older group.

The writers concluded that each group needs the other to really succeed. The younger group needs the steadier hand and general business knowledge of the older group, and the older group needs the content knowledge, inventiveness, and energy of the younger group.

✳ ✳ ✳

Kupperschmidt, B. R. (2000). Tips to help you recruit, manage, and keep
    Generation X employees. *Nursing Management, 31*(3), 58–60.

With Generation X entering the workforce, the old way of managing needs to change, according to the author, who suggested some tips for effective hiring and retention. First, free employees by giving them latitude, control, autonomy, trust, and space. They appreciate and respond well to that type of environment. Second, value their involvement and get them to participate in the organization's decision making because feeling involved is critical to this generation. Third, give recognition where it is due and more frequently than might be given to other generational groups – this generation wants frequent feedback, and, the author argued, recognition is a form of feedback. Fourth, ask for opinions and perspectives from younger employees because they need to feel that they are heard and appreciated to be willing to stay.

The article went on to describe work published by Claire Raines. Raines had cautioned managers not to assume that all employees are alike, to be aware of stereotypes and labels, to be as flexible as possible with work schedules and policies, to actively develop younger workers, to "lighten up," and to "walk your talk."

The author continued with a report on Bruce Tulgan's findings and recommendations. Tulgan interviewed eighty-five Generation X employees and found that they seek jobs that provide marketable skills, knowledge at the vanguard of progress, creative challenges, and relationships with mentors. In exchange for tangible rewards, they sought organizations that recognize employees for the daily value they add. The author provided additional tips on recruiting, orientation, and performance appraisals.

Kupperschmidt completed the article by suggesting that managers responsible for directing Generation X employees don't insist employees stay until official quitting time if the day's work is done; don't keep tabs on when employees arrive and leave; don't give insincere or gratuitous praise; don't give vague instructions when you have specific expectations; and don't inundate employees with wordy instruction manuals and tips for using common technology.

✳✳✳

Losyk, B. (1997). Generation X: What are they like? *Current, 39*(2), 9–13.

Using interviews and reviews of current literature, Losyk looked at current and projected trends in the beliefs, values, and attitudes of Generation X. Current generational trends indicate that Generation X has fewer numbers than the Baby Boomer generation. It was believed that Generation X possessed a more negative view of the world than did previous generations. Generation X was more diverse than other generations. Members of Generation X exhibited less loyalty and commitment to organizations and wanted to keep their career options open. They were technologically literate, wanted an element of fun in their work, and often questioned the boss. The author suggested that in the future Generation X will contribute to the evolution of better race relations, shorter workweeks, greater entrepreneurship, e-commerce business interests, and the establishment of new political parties.

✳✳✳

Manolis, C., Levin, A. A., & Dahlstrom, R. (1997). Generation X scale: Creation and validation. *Educational & Psychological Measurement, 57*(4), 666.

In this study the authors used Douglas Copland's novel, *Generation X,* to develop a scale for measuring the attitudes of Generation Xers (people in their mid-twenties at the time the study was conducted). The resulting scale measured attitudes toward older people in society, parents, jobs, and shopping. The authors compared these attitudes to the attitudes of the Baby Boomer generation. The study's findings showed that Generation Xers have more negative attitudes toward jobs, parents, and yuppies than their Baby Boomer counterparts. The Generation X population also showed a more negative attitude toward shopping than Baby Boomers. The authors argued that the results of this study indicated that Generation X can be classified as a unique generation with distinct attitudes.

***

Martin, G., Staines, H., & Pate, J. (1998). Linking job security and career
   development in a new psychological contract. *Human Resource Management Journal, 8*(3), 20–40.

   This longitudinal research looked at the relationship between the
psychological work contract and training in a Scottish-based textiles company. The research found that the increased value of training resulted from
employees trying to adjust to a climate of increasing job insecurity by making
themselves more employable. When employees feared losing their jobs, they
wanted more training. Blue-collar employees looked upon training as a way
to keep their jobs in case of layoffs; they believed that the more jobs they
were trained for the more useful they would be to the company and the less
likely they were to be laid off. They didn't look at their training as increasing
their external employability because in many cases the training was so job
specific as to be of little use in another job. White-collar employees looked
upon training as a way to increase their external employability and therefore
their value in the marketplace.

   The implications of this study were as follows: (1) when employer
rhetoric and practice are not consistent, there are negative outcomes; (2) job
security is a key worry for employees, and reduced trust levels are common in
downsized organizations; and (3) the training employees think is useful is not
necessarily what employers think is useful. In conclusion, the research found
that when employees believe that the training they receive wasn't what the
organization promised, the psychological contract between the employee and
the employer is damaged further.

***

Munk, N. (1999). Finished at forty. *Fortune, 139*(2), 50–66.

   In this article Munk described the cultural shifts happening in the
workforce today when age becomes a factor in hiring, promoting, and firing
employees. It's those over forty who are concerned, he reported. Demographically, there are more employees in the workforce over forty than under
forty. One challenge the over-forty group has is keeping up with the skills
needed by today's workforce. Younger employees are more technologically
savvy, for example, forcing older employees to keep on top of new skills
before old skills become obsolete. Another factor in this cultural shift is the
difference in attitudes between older and younger employees. The younger
employee mind-set may be more in line with where many organizations are

headed, the writer argued. More and more companies are putting younger employees on the fast track. This frustrates older employees who have "done their time" to achieve the position they occupy. If let go, older employees find it difficult to get back into the work environment because younger employees are taking up their pool of potential positions. The article also reported an increase in age-discrimination lawsuits brought by workers over forty.

❋ ❋ ❋

Ohlott, P. J., & Eastman, L. J. (1994). *Age differences in developmental job experiences: Evidence of a gray ceiling?* Paper presented at the meeting of the Academy of Management, Dallas, TX.

Ohlott and Eastman investigated whether or not developmental job experiences for managers vary with age. The authors used the Developmental Challenge Profile, an instrument that assesses components of jobs that foster managerial learning. Managers from various business and organizational levels completed the instrument to help test the authors' hypothesis that older managers experience fewer job challenges than younger managers.

Ohlott and Eastman's findings had important implications for both younger and older managers. Younger managers reported less support and encouragement from their immediate bosses. This added stress because bosses didn't give young managers advice and feedback for modeling executive behaviors, nor did they pass on skills and strategies necessary for coping with the problems faced in an extremely challenging job. Findings suggested that there are several advantages to establishing mentoring programs between older and younger managers. For younger and less experienced managers, the authors argued, a relationship with a senior mentor would provide younger managers with the means to gather information and support from someone other than the immediate boss. A mentoring program could also create new and challenging roles for senior employees, capitalizing on their knowledge and experience.

In contrast to younger managers, senior managers appeared to have social support but fewer challenging tasks and responsibilities. Older managers also reported learning less on the job than younger managers and that their jobs were less developmental. The authors suggested that organizations plan job changes and assignments for senior employees to help avoid the stagnation that accompanies a career plateau. Growth in an organization refers to the development and utilization of new skills, abilities, and attitudes, the authors maintained, and doesn't necessarily require a promotion. Therefore, organizations should promote personal growth and development for managers (especially older managers) throughout their tenure by creating new and challenging assignments.

Organizations should ensure that promotions, cross-functional transfers, and job rotations are given not only to young high-potential managers but also to seasoned managers, the authors wrote. These assignments give employees a path to broaden their skills. Additional developmental opportunities include temporary assignments, task forces, and troubleshooting assignments. Organizations can also involve older managers in start-up and turnaround assignments.

✳ ✳ ✳

Raines, C. (1997). *Beyond Generation X: A practical guide for managers.* Menlo Park, CA: Crisp Publications, 120 pages.

Raines has previously defined Generation X as having been born between 1960 and 1980, but she has said that Generation X's first official birth year was 1965, the year the U.S. birthrate dropped below four million.

Raines covered several topics in her book, including the difference in socialization of the Baby Boomers and Generation X, how the Boomers changed the workforce, what it was like growing up in the 1970s and 1980s, the Generation X work ethic, challenges facing parents of Gen Xers, and what Generation X wants from its managers.

In the 1970s Baby Boomers became the majority in most companies. They made up a workforce that demanded much of the employer and of themselves, Raines reported, with a collective economic power that surpassed the gross national product of most countries. For much of their early working life they were trapped in either a slow economy or a recession. Boomers were willing to "pay their dues" and study the politics of their organizations. They slowly made their way up the corporate ladder by working long hours and talking with the right people. By the early 1980s they were well established and began to have a profound effect on American society. They were the primary force behind new business practices such as participative management, flattened pyramids, employee involvement, quality circles, team building, and empowerment. At the same time, many Baby Boomers faced reengineering, downsizing, and their own mid-life issues.

Generation X was socialized differently from the Baby Boomers, Raines reported. Their formative years included a rocky economy, the Me Decade (which was centered on the Baby Boomers), outdated schools, latchkey supervision, increasingly sexual and violent television content, fallen heroes, broken homes, and lowered expectations. The news characterized the world they would inherit: a depleted ozone layer, overcrowding, starvation, soaring divorce rates, AIDS, gangs, crime, date rape, and waste. Added to this was the awareness that Generation X would have the financial burden of supporting the Baby Boomers at retirement through Social Security payments without much hope that Social Security would last long enough to benefit their own generation at retirement.

This environment gave rise to a generation Raines described as wanting a lifestyle with more balance – working to live, not living to work. Raines characterized the Generation X work ethic as including self-reliance, skepticism, financial savvy, balance, commitment reluctance, lack of attention to authority, blurred life-stage boundaries, knowledge of technology, and acceptance of diversity. The author suggested that Gen Xers are attracted, retained, and motivated by organizations that are characterized by appreciation, flexibility, teamwork, development, involvement, enjoyment, and credibility.

***

Rapp, J. (1999). Managing Generation X: As employees, as customers. *Office Systems, 16*(8), 14–18.

The author suggested that anyone supervising a member of Generation X will be more likely to succeed if he or she (1) clearly defines the job, (2) establishes how results will be measured, (3) provides constant feedback, and (4) sets up levels of accomplishment. Members of this workplace generation prefer honesty, information, training, responsibility, autonomy, feedback, and fewer rules. They are usually willing to express their opinion when others might not, they expect their bosses to be as straightforward with them as they are with their bosses, and they neither expect nor endorse traditional manifestations of company loyalty.

***

Robinson, S., Kraatz, M., & Rousseau, D. (1994). Changing obligations and the psychological contract: A longitudinal study. *Academy of Management Journal, 37*, 137–152.

This study examined how the psychological contract that employees feel exists between them and their organization changes over time. The sample was from the 1987 alumni of an MBA degree program. This sample was surveyed twice (in 1987 and in 1989), and the results showed that the subjects believed that employers have obligations to employees in the areas of rapid advancement, high pay, pay based on performance, training, long-term job security, career development, and support with personal problems. The level of obligation attributed to the employer was higher in the 1989 survey than in the 1987 survey, and the level of obligation attributed to the employee was lower in 1989 than in 1987. The results indicated that employees' perceived obligations to their employers decreased over time, while the obligations employees attributed to employers increased over time.

✳✳✳

Salopek, J. J. (2000). The young and the rest of us. *Training & Development, 54*, 26–30.

This article focused on the intricacies of training both older and younger workers. It referred to consultants from a management-training firm concentrating on generational issues, who suggested that when planning to train younger workers, trainers and designers should do or attend to the following:

- clarify why the training is important, how the training fits into the company goals, and how the training will benefit the learner
- find ways to assure that the training is entertaining and experiential
- provide one-on-one time so the training has a personalized feeling
- provide feedback in a timely way
- assure workers that the training is participative, with new activities every ten to fifteen minutes
- create safe environments so participants can speak their minds
- clarify who is in charge and set more ground rules than would be necessary with older workers
- allow the participants to learn through interaction and collaboration.

When designing training for older employees, consultants recommended that trainers and designers:

- center the training on the learner
- assure workers that the training is positive, and clearly show the benefits of change
- clarify from the trainee's perspective why the training is important
- find ways to make sure the training is comfortable physically and emotionally
- reduce the stress level of the training, especially during testing
- incorporate the learners' experiences
- provide space for disagreement and discussion.

***

Smith, J. W., & Clurman, A. (1997). *Rocking the ages.* New York: Harper Business, 336 pages.

    In this book two members of the Yankelovich research firm mined databases to provide marketing information about three generational groups: Matures (1909–1945), Baby Boomers (1946–1964), and Generation Xers (1965–present). This text provided marketing professionals with information about each target audience's buying patterns, demographic characteristics, and marketing preferences. It also provided general descriptive information about each generation. The book incorporated both empirical data and case studies to help marketers understand the texture of each generation.

***

Swoboda, F. (1999, Sept. 1). Upward mobility outranks job security in survey of young workers. *The Washington Post*, p. A9.

    This article reported the results of a survey that found that young workers value job security less than advancement opportunities. Young workers believed their employers were not providing high enough salaries or enough room for professional growth. Young workers planned to work at between two and ten organizations during their lifetimes and sought opportunities to update their skills and education. Education seemed to be the key to success for younger workers. Those without college degrees struggled to find full-time employment, while those with degrees found full-time permanent jobs more easily.

***

Tornow, W. (1988). Contract redesign. *Personnel Administrator*, *34*(10), 97–101.

    Because organizations have restructured to align themselves with changes in the world of business and in how employees are led, Tornow argued, the employee-employer contract must also change. The old employment contract resulted from the factors that had historically influenced organizations. Businesses were predictable and stable, population growth was steady, and long-range strategic planning was common. The organization considered its workforce permanent, which influenced personnel programs and practices. Both the organization and the employee regarded their relationship as a long-term one that valued loyalty and commitment.

    The author contended that organizations have now had to function in a different context. They have become less predictable and stable, requiring more frequent and significant adjustments for "long-range" planning. Reorganizations, downsizing, mergers, and acquisitions have replaced stability and predictability. Employment requirements have become more dynamic, with many employees now part-time or temporary. Employee loyalty and commitment are not the same, and job enrichment, participation, and performance/compensation contracting have become important compensation planning tools. Tornow concluded that past human resources management strategies no longer work because of downsizing, mergers, acquisitions, layoffs, and the effect those factors have had on job security and changes in company loyalty.

✳✳✳

Tunnicliffe, A. M. (1997). Helping Generation Xers decipher protocol. *HR Focus, 74*(12), 5.

The focus of this article was on molding Generation X members into successful employees. The author outlined seven tips on corporate etiquette that will be helpful to Generation X employees:

1. show respect and deference to colleagues

2. rise respectfully for social introductions

3. use a positive handshake rather than a casual wave

4. work on improving conversational skills

5. pay close attention to grooming and attire

6. learn how to effectively navigate business and social events

7. present a polished image in written communication.

✳✳✳

Wagschal, P. H. (1995). Identities, technology distinguish the learning habits of generations: Silence, Boomers and Generation X should be trained differently. *San Diego Business Journal, 16*(32), 24–25.

In this article Wagschal contended that it's critically important to focus on the age of students, as well as the generational identities and technological perspectives that have shaped students. This article defined the generations currently in the workplace: the Silent Generation (1925–1942), Baby Boomers (1943–1960), and Thirteeners/Generation X (1961–1981). As learning opportunities are developed for adults, the author suggested that developers of training programs need to take into account the vastly different experiences each generation has had regarding the growth of technology. Each generation has developed differences in learning style, worldviews, and critical-thinking skills as technologies emerged during its life span.

✳✳✳

Watkins, C. (1999). Grads to grannies, managing the generation gap. *Food Management, 34*(9), 31–35.

 Watkins addressed two workplace trends: the growing youth labor force and the increase in seniors in the workforce. The author argued that it's the manager's responsibility to capitalize on employees' strengths and to help them develop in those areas where they are weakest. The author suggested that managers avoid stereotyping and understand that they may harbor age biases. Managers should make expectations clear and standard for all employees, regardless of age. Managers must foster mutual respect among workers and should be aware of the different levels of work and life experience workers bring to a job. Managers should do as much as they can to create workplace environments that provide and address the benefits and workplace issues that are important to each employee age group, and they should work to provide more flexible work schedules. Finally, managers should take generational differences into account regarding work ethics and accordingly modify their management style.

 The most important step in managing this diversity of generations, the author concluded, was for managers to accept that the different generations in the workplace do not necessarily share the same work ethic, interests, and expectations.

✳✳✳

Withers, P. (1998). What makes Gen X employees tick? *BC Business, 26*(3), 2–6.

 This article addressed the question of what managers need to know to lead Generation X employees. This generation entered the workforce during a recession, so they frequently took jobs unequal to their skills and training and that offered little opportunity for promotion. The author reported that Generation X workers had the perception that older Generation Xers were being passed over because employers were interested in the younger, more technically adept Generation X employees. These experiences and perceptions created a group of cynical, unmotivated, and skill-hungry employees. Therefore, to retain and develop younger Generation X employees, employers should provide more training and advancement to assuage their desire for more skills. Employers should also focus on making work more meaningful to this group by allowing such employees more latitude in defining their own work, providing them greater autonomy in their jobs, offering flexible work hours as an option, and offering social outlets in the workplace.

✳✳✳

Woodward, N. H. (1999). The coming of the managers. *HR Magazine, 44*(3), 74–80.

This article examined how members of the Generation X group act as managers. Through a series of studies, researchers found that Generation X managers were managing others the way they themselves would like to be managed. This included giving employees the desired results and limitations of projects and then leaving them alone to complete the work, sharing credit, working with employees as a team, providing feedback when needed, and rewarding employees for a job well done.

The author noted challenges Generation X managers faced. Baby Boom generation employees reported frustration when receiving feedback from someone younger, even if that person was their boss. Gen Xers were frustrated with organizational systems that made it difficult or impossible for them to provide immediate rewards, and they had trouble managing employees who didn't fulfill expectations. The greatest challenge for Gen X managers was understanding the difference between the way they managed (and wanted to be managed) and how their Baby Boomer employees wanted to be managed.

✳ ✳ ✳

List of World Wide Web Sites
Pertaining to the Subject of Generation X[†]

Because this sourcebook of annotated bibliographies focuses on emerging leaders and generational differences, and because one of the primary differences between emerging leaders and other generations is each group's level of comfort with computer technology (including the Internet and the World Wide Web), we have included in this section of the book a guide to World Wide Web sites that have particular relevance to an examination of generational differences – particularly as they pertain to organizational, social, and political issues.

Some of the more interesting and contemporary writing on these topics can only be found on the Web. We caution the reader to view all of these sites with a critical eye. Not all Web-based publications subject themselves to rigorous review, and many Web-based sources shift, vanish, or become moribund from neglect. We have included sites we think are useful either as sources of information or as gateways to other sources of information. The sites are listed in alphabetical order and were available for browsing at the date noted.

[†]Traditionally, CCL Press Sourcebooks, particularly annotated bibliographies, have only included selected printed works for several reasons. First, published work is generally subjected to some sort of evaluation process (peer review for academic journals and presses, professional editorial review for trade books and the general press), which provides some measure of quality. Second, published sources are a stable medium – copies can be requested from libraries, booksellers, or publishers. The authors of CCL Press Sourcebooks select sources that are not only relevant to the subject but that are accessible to readers who want to pursue their investigation into the topic. That said, it's apparent that the Internet, and in particular the World Wide Web, has become an important channel for published work that may not appear in traditional print media.

4BabyBoomers.com. Accessed June 2001 from the World Wide Web.
http://4babyboomers.4anything.com/
   This Web site directory contained links and content for and about Baby
Boomers.

The American Association of Retired Persons (AARP). Accessed June 2001
from the World Wide Web.
http://www.aarp.org
   This site contained numerous topics regarding help, support, and
interests for those fifty years of age and older.

American Demographics. Accessed June 2001 from the World Wide Web.
http://www.demographics.com
   This site contained the *American Demographics* magazine and links to
a wide variety of resources.

Baby Boomer Headquarters (BBHQ). Accessed July 2001 from the World
Wide Web.
http://www.bbhq.com/
   The Baby Boomer Headquarters provided content and chat rooms for
those interested in the Baby Boom generation.

Boomer Café. Accessed July 2001 from the World Wide Web.
http://www.boomercafe.com/
   Boomer Café was an online magazine for America's Baby Boomers.

The Boomer Initiative. Accessed June 2001 from the World Wide Web.
http://www.babyboomers.com/
   The site of this nonprofit organization focused on the challenges and
potential of the American generation born between 1946 and 1964.

Boomers International. Accessed June 2001 from the World Wide Web.
http://boomersint.org/
   This site hosted a community outlook for Baby Boomers.

Delphi's "The BabyBOOMers." Accessed July 2001 from the World Wide
Web.
http://www.delphi.com/boomer/
   This site provided message boards and live chat rooms catering to
people interested in Baby Boom generation topics.

The Fourth Turning. Accessed June 2001 from the World Wide Web.
http://www.fourthturning.com
    This site focused on the book *Fourth Turning* and research by its authors Neil Howe and Bill Strauss. It contained content regarding generational archetypes and a discussion column.

Gen X Café. Accessed July 2001 from the World Wide Web.
http://www.geocities.com/SouthBeach/Sands/1919/
    Gen X Café offered a place on the Internet for Gen Xers to speak their minds.

Generation Forward. Accessed June 2001 from the World Wide Web.
http://www.generationforward.com/home.htm
    The site of this recruitment, training, and management consulting firm provided company information and an overview of what motivates Generation X workers.

The Generational Inquiry Group. Accessed June 2001 from the World Wide Web.
http://www.millennials.com
    Another site based on the work of authors Neil Howe and William Strauss, with discussions about what they call *Millennials* – the generation of Americans following Generation X.

Growing Up Digital. Accessed June 2001 from the World Wide Web.
http://www.growingupdigital.com
    This site featured the work of Don Tapscott, author of the book *Growing Up Digital: The Rise of the New Generation.*

The International Association of Baby Boomers Plus! Accessed June 2001 from the World Wide Web.
http://www.boomersassoc.com
    The site of this commercial association focused on services and information for Americans born between 1977 and 1994.

The National Association of Baby Boomers. Accessed June 2001 from the World Wide Web.
http://www.babyboomers.org
    The site of this not-for-profit organization offered membership to people wanting to form a lobbying and information network devoted to Baby Boomer issues, plus a nascent nostalgia discussion.

New Strategist Publications. Accessed June 2001 from the World Wide Web. http://www.newstrategist.com
     This reference book publisher's site provided samples and for-purchase extracts of its publications dealing with trends in consumer marketing data, census information, and other demographic sources.

Peel. Accessed June 2001 from the World Wide Web. http://www.peelworld.com/
     This online magazine featured articles on a variety of topics of interest to Generation X.

Generations at Work. Accessed June 2001 from the World Wide Web. http://www.generationsatwork.com
     This site included issues of the author Claire Raines's *Generations: A Newsletter for Managers* and links to other generation-related products.

Rainmaker Thinking. Accessed June 2001 from the World Wide Web. http://www.rainmakerthinking.com
     This research, training, and consulting firm hosts this site focused on the working lives of people born after 1963.

Adam Rifkin's Generation X Page. Accessed June 2001 from the World Wide Web.
http://www.cs.caltech.edu/~adam/lead/genx.html
     This Web page included more than seventy-five links to sites that might be of interest to Generation Xers.

Seniors Organization. Accessed June 2001 from the World Wide Web. http://www.seniors.com
     This site contained content and links to organizations that might be of interest to older (age fifty-five and up) Americans.

Third Millennium. Accessed June 2001 from the World Wide Web. http://www.thirdmil.org
     This site was sponsored by a national, nonpartisan, not-for-profit political organization looking to organize Generation Xers around the political and policy issues that will affect their futures.

Author Index

Title Index

CENTER FOR CREATIVE LEADERSHIP PUBLICATIONS LIST

NEW RELEASES

IDEAS INTO ACTION GUIDEBOOKS

Ongoing Feedback: How to Get It, How to Use It Kirkland & Manoogian (1998, Stock #400) $8.95*

Reaching Your Development Goals McCauley & Martineau (1998, Stock #401) $8.95

Becoming a More Versatile Learner Dalton (1998, Stock #402) $8.95

Giving Feedback to Subordinates Buron & McDonald-Mann (1999, Stock #403) $8.95*

Three Keys to Development: Using Assessment, Challenge, and Support to Drive Your Leadership
Browning & Van Velsor (1999, Stock #404) $8.95

Feedback That Works: How to Build and Deliver Your Message Weitzel (2000, Stock #405) $8.95*

Communicating Across Cultures Prince & Hoppe (2000, Stock #406) $8.95

Learning From Life: Turning Life's Lessons into Leadership Experience Ruderman & Ohlott
(2000, Stock #407) $8.95

Keeping Your Career on Track: Twenty Success Strategies Chappelow & Leslie (2001, Stock #408) $8.95

Preparing for Development: Making the Most of Formal Leadership Programs Martineau &
Johnson (2001, Stock #409) $8.95

Choosing an Executive Coach Kirkland & Hart (2001, Stock #410) $8.95

Setting Your Development Goals: Start with Your Values Sternbergh & Weitzel (2001, Stock #411) $8.95

Do You Really Need a Team? Kossler & Kanaga (2001, Stock #412) $8.95

The Deep Blue Sea: Rethinking the Source of Leadership Drath (2001, Stock #2068) $27.95

Discovering the Leader in You Lee & King (2001, Stock #2067) $32.95

Emerging Leaders: An Annotated Bibliography Deal, Peterson, & Gailor-Loflin (2001, Stock #352) ... $20.00

Executive Coaching: An Annotated Bibliography Douglas & Morley (2000, Stock #347) $20.00

Executive Selection: Strategies for Success Sessa & Taylor (2000, Stock #2057) $34.95*

The Human Side of Knowledge Management: An Annotated Bibliography Mayer (2000,
Stock #349) $20.00

Leadership Resources: A Guide to Training and Development Tools (8th ed.) Schwartz & Gimbel
(2000, Stock #348) $49.95*

BEST-SELLERS

Breaking Free: A Prescription for Personal and Organizational Change Noer (1997, Stock #271) $25.00

Breaking the Glass Ceiling: Can Women Reach the Top of America's Largest Corporations?
(Updated Edition) Morrison, White, & Van Velsor (1992, Stock #236A) $13.00

The Center for Creative Leadership Handbook of Leadership Development McCauley, Moxley,
& Van Velsor (Eds.) (1998, Stock #201) $75.00*

Choosing 360: A Guide to Evaluating Multi-rater Feedback Instruments for Management
Development Van Velsor, Leslie, & Fleenor (1997, Stock #334) $15.00*

Choosing Executives: A Research Report on the Peak Selection Simulation Deal, Sessa, & Taylor
(1999, Stock #183) $20.00*

Coaching for Action: A Report on Long-term Advising in a Program Context Guthrie (1999,
Stock #181) $20.00*

The Complete Inklings: Columns on Leadership and Creativity Campbell (1999, Stock #343) $20.00

Eighty-eight Assignments for Development in Place Lombardo & Eichinger (1989, Stock #136) $15.00*

Enhancing 360-degree Feedback for Senior Executives: How to Maximize the Benefits and
Minimize the Risks Kaplan & Palus (1994, Stock #160) $7.50*

Executive Selection: A Research Report on What Works and What Doesn't Sessa, Kaiser,
Taylor, & Campbell (1998, Stock #179) $30.00*

Feedback to Managers (3rd Edition) Leslie & Fleenor (1998, Stock #178) $20.00*

Four Essential Ways that Coaching Can Help Executives Witherspoon & White (1997, Stock #175) $10.00

High Flyers: Developing the Next Generation of Leaders McCall (1997, Stock #293) $27.95

How to Design an Effective System for Developing Managers and Executives Dalton &
Hollenbeck (1996, Stock #158) $15.00*

If I'm In Charge Here, Why Is Everybody Laughing? Campbell (1984, Stock #205) $9.95*

If You Don't Know Where You're Going You'll Probably End Up Somewhere Else Campbell (1974, Stock #203) $9.95*

Internalizing Strengths: An Overlooked Way of Overcoming Weaknesses in Managers Kaplan (1999, Stock #182) $15.00

International Success: Selecting, Developing, and Supporting Expatriate Managers Wilson & Dalton (1998, Stock #180) $15.00*

Leadership and Spirit Moxley (1999, Stock #2035) $35.00

The Lessons of Experience: How Successful Executives Develop on the Job McCall, Lombardo, & Morrison (1988, Stock #211) $28.00

Making Common Sense: Leadership as Meaning-making in a Community of Practice Drath & Palus (1994, Stock #156) $15.00

Maximizing the Value of 360-degree Feedback Tornow, London, & CCL Associates (1998, Stock #295) $45.00*

Perspectives on Dialogue: Making Talk Developmental for Individuals and Organizations Dixon (1996, Stock #168) $20.00

Positive Turbulence: Developing Climates for Creativity, Innovation, and Renewal Gryskiewicz (1999, Stock #2031) $35.00

Preventing Derailment: What To Do Before It's Too Late Lombardo & Eichinger (1989, Stock #138) $25.00

Selected Research on Work Team Diversity Ruderman, Hughes-James, & Jackson (Eds.) (1996, Stock #326) $24.95

Should 360-degree Feedback Be Used Only for Developmental Purposes? Bracken, Dalton, Jako, McCauley, Pollman, with Preface by Hollenbeck (1997, Stock #335) $15.00*

Take the Road to Creativity and Get Off Your Dead End Campbell (1977, Stock #204) $9.95*

Twenty-two Ways to Develop Leadership in Staff Managers Eichinger & Lombardo (1990, Stock #144) $15.00

BIBLIOGRAPHIES

Formal Mentoring Programs in Organizations: An Annotated Bibliography Douglas (1997, Stock #332) $20.00

Geographically Dispersed Teams: An Annotated Bibliography Sessa, Hansen, Prestridge, & Kossler (1999, Stock #346) $20.00

High-Performance Work Organizations: Definitions, Practices, and an Annotated Bibliography Kirkman, Lowe, & Young (1999, Stock #342) $20.00

Management Development through Job Experiences: An Annotated Bibliography McCauley & Brutus (1998, Stock #337) $10.00

Selecting International Executives: A Suggested Framework and Annotated Bibliography London & Sessa (1999, Stock #345) $20.00

Selection at the Top: An Annotated Bibliography Sessa & Campbell (1997, Stock #333) $20.00*

Succession Planning: An Annotated Bibliography Eastman (1995, Stock #324) $20.00*

Using 360-degree Feedback in Organizations: An Annotated Bibliography Fleenor & Prince (1997, Stock #338) $15.00*

Workforce Reductions: An Annotated Bibliography Hickok (1999, Stock #344) $20.00

SPECIAL PACKAGES

Executive Selection Package (Stock #710C; includes 157, 164, 179, 180, 183, 333, 345, 2057) $100.00

Feedback Guidebook Package (Stock #724; includes 400, 403, 405) $17.95

Human Resources Professionals Information Package (Stock #717C; includes 136, 158, 179, 180, 181, 201, 324, 334, 348—includes complimentary copy of guidebook 407) $150.00

Personal Growth, Taking Charge, and Enhancing Creativity (Stock #231; includes 203, 204, 205) ... $25.00

The 360 Collection (Stock #720C; includes 160, 178, 295, 334, 335, 338—includes complimentary copy of guidebook 400) $100.00

Discounts are available. Please write for a Resources catalog. Address your request to: Publication, Center for Creative Leadership, P.O. Box 26300, Greensboro, NC 27438-6300, 336-545-2810, or fax to 336-282-3284. Purchase your publications from our online bookstore at **www.ccl.org/ publications**. All prices subject to change.

*Indicates publication is also part of a package.

ORDER FORM

Or e-mail your order via the Center's online bookstore at www.ccl.org

Name _____ Title _____

Organization _____

Mailing Address _____
(street address required for mailing)

City/State/Zip _____

Telephone _____ FAX _____
(telephone number required for UPS mailing)

Quantity	Stock No.	Title	Unit Cost	Amount

CCL's Federal ID Number
is 237-07-9591.

Subtotal	
Shipping and Handling (U.S. shipping rate $4 for 1st book, $0.95 for each additional book; International shipping rate $20 for 1st book, $5 for each additional book)	
NC residents add 6% sales tax; CA residents add 7.5% sales tax; CO residents add 6% sales tax	
TOTAL	

METHOD OF PAYMENT
(ALL orders for less than $100 must be PREPAID.)

❏ Check or money order enclosed (payable to Center for Creative Leadership).

❏ Purchase Order No. _____ (Must be accompanied by this form.)

❏ Charge my order, plus shipping, to my credit card:
      ❏ American Express ❏ Discover ❏ MasterCard ❏ Visa

ACCOUNT NUMBER:_____ EXPIRATION DATE: MO.____ YR.____

NAME OF ISSUING BANK: _____

SIGNATURE _____

❏ Please put me on your mailing list.

Publication • Center for Creative Leadership • P.O. Box 26300
Greensboro, NC 27438-6300
336-545-2810 • FAX 336-282-3284

8/01

Client Priority Code: R

fold here

PLACE
STAMP
HERE

CENTER FOR CREATIVE LEADERSHIP
PUBLICATION
P.O. Box 26300
Greensboro, NC 27438-6300